Calligraphy *for*
SWIFTIES

Bluestone Books
www.bluestonebooks.co

ISBN: 978-1-965636-16-9 (trade paperback)

Printed in the United States of America
10 9 8 7 6 5 4 3 2 1

Design by Melissa Gerber
Illustrations used under license by Shutterstock

Calligraphy *for* SWIFTIES

Hand-Lettering Practice with Taylor Swift's Favorite Words

By Sophia Ivy

BLUEST●NE
BOOKS

CONTENTS

CALLIGRAPHY *for* SWIFTIES

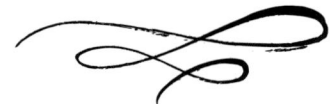

Take a seat at Taylor Swift's writing desk. Glancing around, you'll spy stacks of typewriter paper straight from *The Tortured Poets Department.* You'll eye quill pens dipped in black ink having scrawled "Sad Beautiful Tragic" songs, glitter gel pens that came out when "Today Was a Fairytale," and pages smudged with teardrops and fountain pen ink when it was a "Cruel Summer." Every Taylor era is marked by how she wields her pen-shaped sword, to the point where any self-respecting Swiftie can belt out a bridge with just one look at lettering that reminds them of her *reputation.*

Channel your Swiftie energy to create your own "fearless" script. In this lettering devotional to Taylor Swift, you can capture the energy of some of her most influential eras with fun calligraphy styles. Discover the best ways to recreate five dazzling lettering styles with simple calligraphy tips and tricks. Each font will transport you to the mood of a different era: Carla Sans is giving *Fearless*, Sudestada is turning up for *Speak Now*, Engraver's Old English is checking your *reputation*, Love Pro wants to be your *Lover*, and IM Fell DW Pica Italic is harking back to *folklore* and *evermore*.

Choose a calligraphy era and use the easy-to-follow practice pages to become a lettering mastermind. You'll find simple steps to recreate the lettering style, with helpful tips along the way, as well as practice pages of words and phrases that will have you putting the record needle on her albums or turning up the volume on your earbuds. With these enchanting calligraphy styles in your quiver, you can become "The Archer" of your lettering projects and make the most of your "quill pens" 'til the ink runs dry.

Use the lettering styles to handwrite personal letters, invitations, signs, and even wall art. Host parties to sip and script your way through all of T-Swift's albums. But most of all, be fearless! Let the swooping and sloping of the lines on your page relax you while the thrill of making something beautiful inspires you. Enjoy *Calligraphy for Swifties* and transform your Swiftie status into something "Gorgeous" to show off and share!

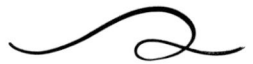

GRAB *a* PEN...

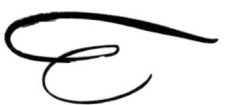

In Taylor's world, her pen is her voice, her heart, and her sword. With just a pen, you can make something beautiful, share love and laughs, make your voice heard, and feel empowered. But before you can fully express yourself on ink and paper, you'll want to know the basics of calligraphy, how to use the pen to your advantage, and how to treat it properly. While you can enchant any pen to write in the lettering style of your choice, certain pens are better for certain styles. You'll come across thin brush pens for elegant, wandering script; thick brush pens for bold and swooping statements; and pens with a firm chisel nib—which is to say that it'll give you a firm and angular stroke for big impact.

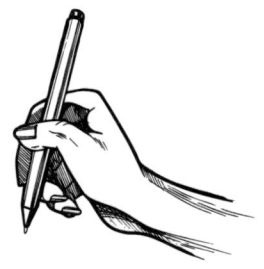

BRUSH PENS

Brush pens have flexible tips. You'll make the most of these pens in many calligraphy styles. A **thin (or small) brush pen** will be perfect when you're ready to *Speak Now*, while a **thick (or big) brush pen** will let you pull off *folklore* and *evermore* moods. Consider these pointers as you bring your pen to paper.

LETTERING CLUES

GRIP: Don't kill your pen. Use a gentle but steady grip on your pen and resist the urge to push the tip aggressively into the paper.

ANGLE: Keep your pen at a 45-degree angle when you write, rather than pressing directly down.

UPSTROKES: These lines create the thin strokes in lettering and occur when you bring the pen up on the page. You just need to put the tip of the pen on the page to create this effect as you draw your line. "Smooshing" the pen so that the tip bends will create a heavier stroke.

DOWNSTROKES: These lines create the thick strokes in lettering and occur when you bring the pen down on the page. Here, you can press more deeply so that the tip bends and creates a heavier stroke.

OVERTURNS: The motion you make when creating an arch, like an "n." Start with a low-pressure upstroke to create a thin line. As you make the arc, apply heavy pressure on the downstroke to create a thick line. Practice this until you have a fluid motion.

UNDERTURNS: The motion you make when creating a well, like a "u." Start with a heavy-pressure downstroke to create a thick line. At the mid-point of the well or u-shape, lighten the pressure on the up-stroke to create a thin line. Practice this until you have a fluid motion.

OVALS: Useful for Os and Cs, this shape requires a combination of turns. Beginning at 2 o'clock, apply light pressure to create an upstroke. Move counterclockwise and transition to a thick downstroke at 12 o'clock. At 6'clock, switch back to an upstroke until you complete the oval or finish the "c."

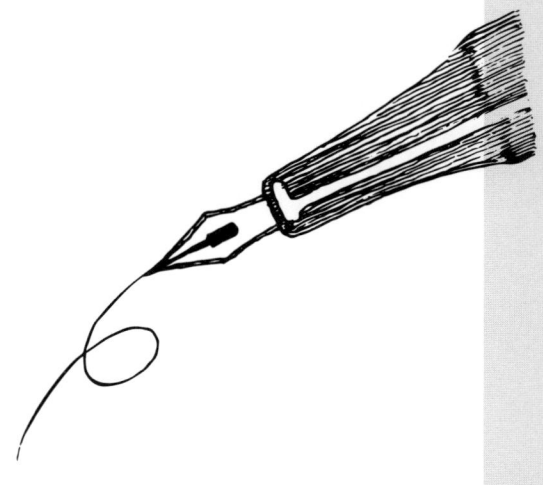

PRACTICING WITH BRUSH PENS

UPSTROKES

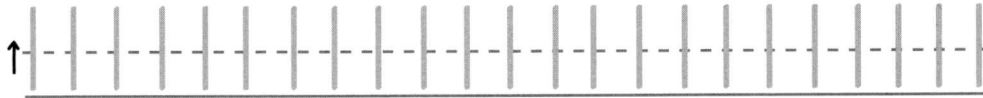

DOWNSTROKES

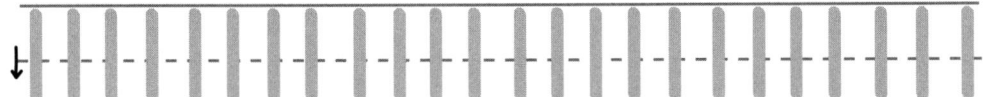

OVERTURNS

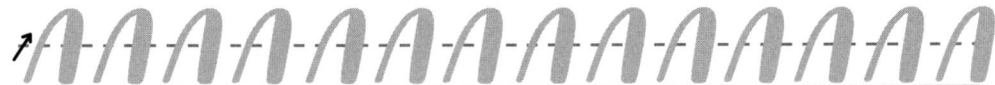

UNDERTURNS

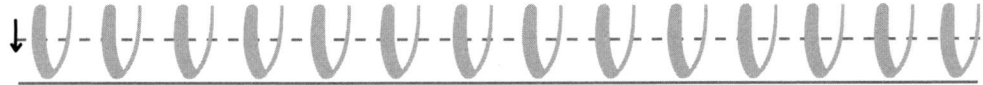

CHISEL PENS

Chisel calligraphy pens have long, firm tips ("nibs") that work well with sharp angles. Use this style pen for traditional calligraphy styles like Engraver's Old English, aka *reputation* calligraphy, or strong and *Fearless* letters. Keep a few things in mind as you get into your narrative.

LETTERING CLUES

GRIP: Use a gentle but steady grip on your pen.

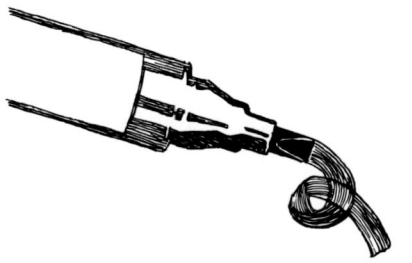

ANGLE: Keep your pen at a 45-degree angle when you write, rather than pressing directly down. In other words, hold the pen so that the pointed edge of the tip is positioned at the 9 o'clock mark. This gives your lettering a clean, angular finish.

UPSTROKES: These lines create the thin strokes in lettering and occur when you bring the pen up on the page. The chisel edge is firm, which allows the upstroke to stay thin.

DOWNSTROKES: These lines create the thick strokes in lettering and occur when you bring the pen down on the page. The firm pen allows you to create thick, angular lines that leave a clean finish.

THIS IS WHY WE CAN'T HAVE NICE THINGS

Try not to be "treacherous" with your calligraphy pens. Replace the caps when you've paused writing so they don't dry out faster than you'd like. Try not to put too much pressure as you write, which can break down the nib or contribute to fraying. When practicing, use tracing paper to extend the life of your pen. When creating your "Version" of anything, try out nice paper like laser-jet paper or papers with a smooth finish. Grittier papers like construction paper or textured paper can shorten your pens' lifespans. Your well-loved pens will eventually fray, so be sure to thank them when they do.

PRACTICING WITH CHISEL PENS

DOWNSTROKES

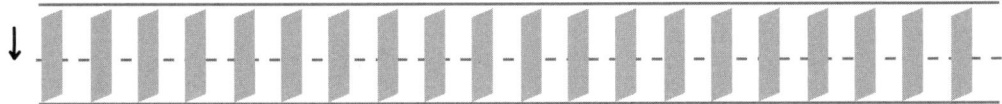

DIAGONALS

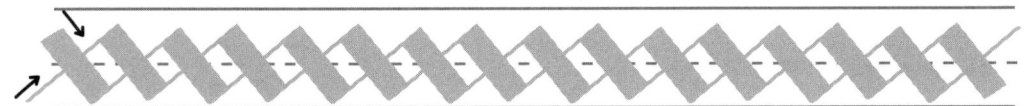

WAVES

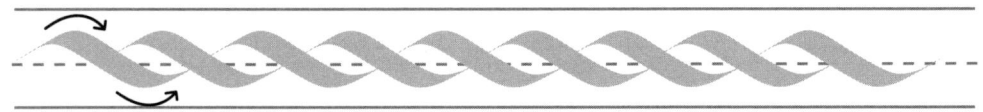

FEARLESS SCRIPT

Calligrapher, Just Say Yes

TAYLOR'S DEBUT ALBUM TOLD COUNTRY LOVERS SHE WAS THERE TO MAKE A NAME FOR HERSELF. BUT *FEARLESS* TOLD THE WORLD THAT SHE BELONGED WITH EVERYONE. The original font on the 2008 album was a clean sans serif style with evenly balanced weight on the lettering strokes, but the 2021 *Taylor's Version* update saw subtle shifts. With thin line strokes on the Es and A, and an exaggerated R, the revised *Fearless* lettering dons an all-new elegance that can only come with maturity.

Fearless lettering isn't careless lettering, and simplicity doesn't mean unintentional. This thoughtful style wants to make itself known while giving off dignity and grace. It's the kind of calligraphy you use to make announcements, to celebrate milestones, and to show off relaxed sophistication. Be fearless in your expression and use this style to elevate your proud moments

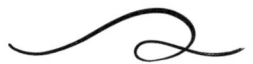

Calligrapher's Desk

STYLE: Carla Sans

FEELS LIKE: *Fearless*

STATEMENT: Sing it loud

PEN: Calligrapher's pen with a 2–3mm chisel nib

CARLA SANS may look easy, but there is a precision to it in the same way that Taylor is precise about even the tiniest details. When making large horizontal strokes and downstrokes with this style, hold your pen at a right angle so that if you just pressed the flat edge to the paper, it would make a horizontal line —. When lettering finer horizontal strokes, as in the middle strokes of the Es, hold your pen so that only the tip of the tip only touches the paper. Use a steady hand with a medium grip when showing off your stylish, courageous voice in this style and have "the best day."

FEAR

A B C D E F G
H I J K L M N
O P Q R S T
U V W X Y Z

LESS

A A A A A A

B B B B B B

C C C C C C

D D D D D D

E E E E E E

F F F F F F

G G G G G G

H H H H H H H

I I I I I I I

J J J J J J J

K K K K K K K

L L L L L L L

M M M M M M M

N N N N N N N

O O O O O O O

P P P P P P P

Q Q Q Q Q Q Q

R R R R R R R

S S S S S S

T T T T T T

U U U U U U

V V V V V V

W W W W W W

X X X X X X

Y Y Y Y Y Y Y

Z Z Z Z Z Z Z

1 1 1 1 1 1 1 1 1 1

2 2 2 2 2 2 2 2 2 2

3 3 3 3 3 3 3 3 3 3

4 4 4 4 4 4 4 4 4 4

5 5 5 5 5 5 5 5 5 5

6 6 6 6 6 6 6 6 6 6

7 7 7 7 7 7 7 7 7 7

8 8 8 8 8 8 8 8 8 8

9 9 9 9 9 9 9 9 9 9

10 10 10 10 10 10 10 10 10 10

FEARLESS

FEARLESS

FEARLESS

FEARLESS

FEARLESS

FEARLESS

THE BEST

DAY

THE BEST

DAY

THE BEST

DAY

TODAY WAS
A FAIRYTALE

TODAY WAS

A FAIRYTALE

TODAY WAS

A FAIRYTALE

YOU BELONG

WITH ME

YOU BELONG

WITH ME

YOU BELONG

WITH ME

IT'S A LOVE STORY. . . .

IT'S A LOVE STORY. . . .

IT'S A LOVE STORY. . . .

WHITE HORSE,

HEART HANDS

WHITE HORSE,

HEART HANDS

WHITE HORSE,

HEART HANDS

MR. PERFECTLY

FINE

MR. PERFECTLY

FINE

MR. PERFECTLY

FINE

KISSING IN THE RAIN

KISSING IN

THE RAIN

KISSING IN

THE RAIN

JUMP

THEN FALL

JUMP

THEN FALL

JUMP

THEN FALL

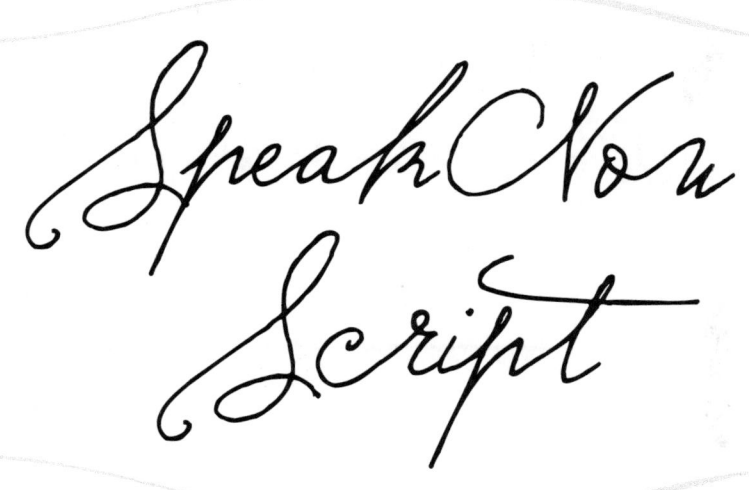

Enchanted to Write You

DON'T UNDERESTIMATE THE DELICATE, FEMININE GRACE OF *SPEAK NOW*. This album captures what Taylor is so good at: being vulnerable and commanding at the same time. The gentle curves of Sudestada lettering fit this gorgeous duality like a glove. This calligraphy style has a gentle sweep and a dreamy quality, perfect for capturing raw honesty and the fairy-tale wonder.

Sudestada's simple elegance lends itself to affectionate notes to friends, party invitations, and love letters alike. Just like Taylor's lyrics that feel plucked from secret diaries, this calligraphy font lets you say what you mean without losing your sense of style. When you want to add beautiful flourishes to even the simplest situations, Sudestada is at your fingertips.

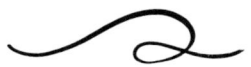

Calligrapher's Desk

STYLE: Sudestada

FEELS LIKE: *Speak Now*

STATEMENT: Be enchanting

PEN: Fine-tip brush pen

CHANNEL the dramatic flair of Taylor's quill-pen lyrics. Sudestada's refined lines begin precisely and end in mischievous flourishes, just like the expressive letters on the cover of *Speak Now*. Hold your fine-tip pen at a comfortable angle to allow the tip to create clean, thin lines. Work smoothly and broadly, keeping your grip loose and your movements controlled. Each letter should be crafted with intention to show the delicate nature of the script.

A B C D E F G H I J
K L M N O P Q R S T
U V W X Y Z

a b c d e f g h i j
k l m n o p q r s t
u v w x y z

A *A* *A* *A* *A* *A* *A* *A*

B *B* *B* *B* *B* *B* *B*

C *C* *C* *C* *C* *C*

D *D* *D* *D* *D* *D*

E *E* *E* *E* *E* *E*

F *F* *F* *F* *F* *F* *F*

𝒢 𝒢 𝒢 𝒢 𝒢 𝒢

ℋ ℋ ℋ ℋ ℋ ℋ

𝒴 𝒴 𝒴 𝒴 𝒴 𝒴

𝒥 𝒥 𝒥 𝒥 𝒥 𝒥

𝒳 𝒳 𝒳 𝒳 𝒳 𝒳

ℒ ℒ ℒ ℒ ℒ ℒ

S S S S S S S

T T T T T T

U U U U U U

V V V V V V

W W W W W

X X X X X X

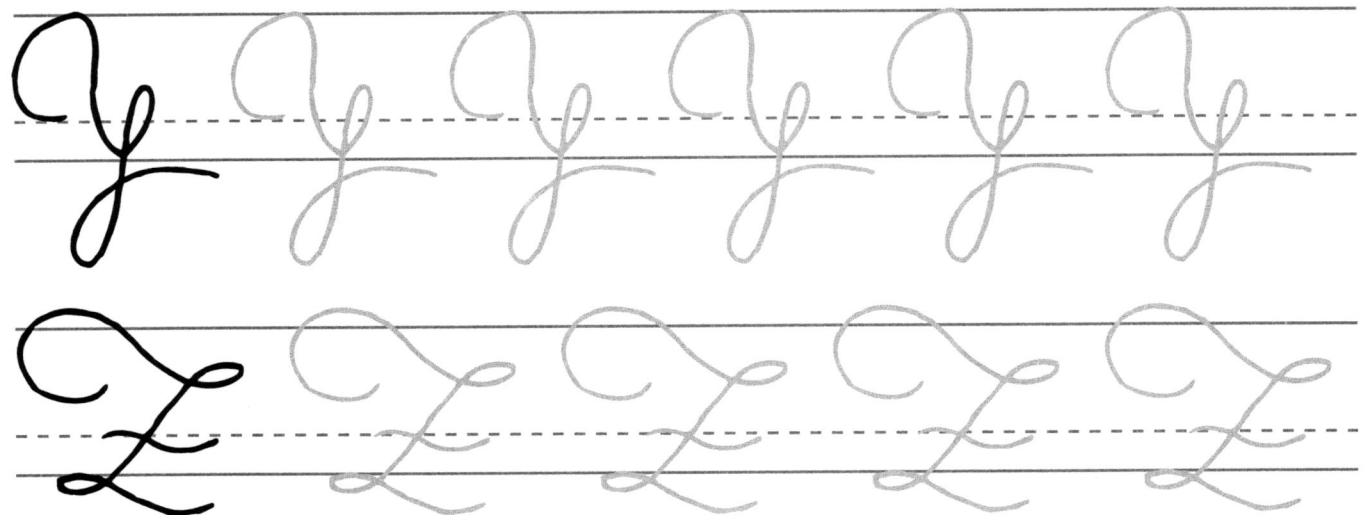

a a a a a a a

b b b b b b

c c c c c c c

d d d d d d

e e e e e e

f f f f f f

g g g g g g g

h h h h h h h

i i i i i i i

j j j j j j j

k k k k k k k

l l l l l l l

m m m m m m

n n n n n n

a a a a a a

p p p p p p

g g g g g g

r r r r r r

s s s s s s

t t t t t t

u u u u u u

v v v v v v

w w w w w w

x x x x x x

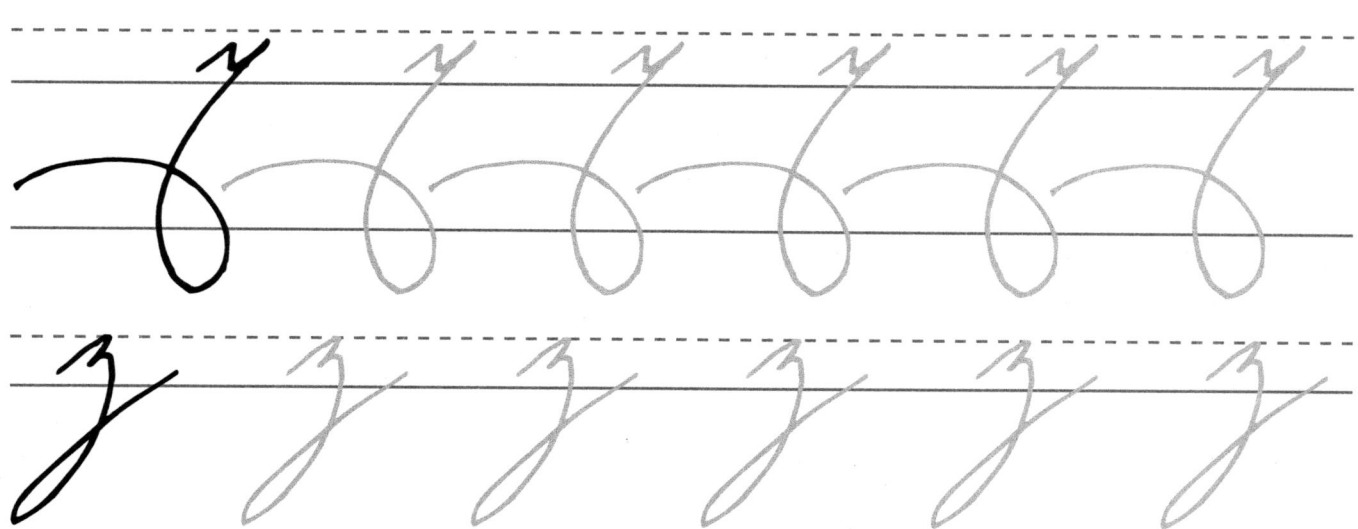

1   1   1   1   1   1   1   1

2   2   2   2   2   2   2   2

3   3   3   3   3   3   3   3

4   4   4   4   4   4   4   4

5   5   5   5   5   5   5   5

6   6   6   6   6   6   6   6

7   7   7   7   7   7   7   7

8   8   8   8   8   8   8   8

9   9   9   9   9   9   9   9

10   10   10   10   10   10   10

Sparks Fly

Sparks Fly

Sparks Fly

Sparks Fly

Sparks Fly

Better Than

Revenge

Better Than

Revenge

Better Than

Revenge

Enchanted to
Meet You

Enchanted to
Meet You

Enchanted to
Meet You

The Story of Us

The Story of Us

The Story of Us

The Story of Us

The Story of Us

Back to December

Back to December

Back to December

Back to December

Back to December

Speak Now

Speak Now

Speak Now

Speak Now

Speak Now

Long Live Taylor

Long Live Taylor

Long Live Taylor

Long Live Taylor

Long Live Taylor

Castles Crumbling

Castles Crumbling

Castles Crumbling

Castles Crumbling

Castles Crumbling

Taylor's Version

Taylor's Version

Taylor's Version

Taylor's Version

Taylor's Version

Never Grow Up

Never Grow Up

Never Grow Up

Never Grow Up

Never Grow Up

reputation script

. . . Ready for It?

NO OTHER ALBUM IN THE TAYLOR-VERSE HAS THE INSTANT RECOGNITION THAT *REPUTATION* COMMANDS. This powerhouse of an album is Taylor at her fiercest, and the calligraphy style that goes along with it is no exception. A take on gothic newsprint lettering, often called "Blackletter," this script is all headlines, all gossip, all fame, all reputation. By supercharging this font with her own attitude, Taylor takes the criticism from the press and makes it her power source.

There's a simplicity in working with this script, but it's also very deliberate. In the same way that Taylor masterminds her clues, plans, and albums, this script is all about intentional, careful detail that makes a statement. Perfect for etching your favorite lyrics, for crafting invitations, or for writing strongly worded letters to the editor to crush gossip, this lettering is powerful. Excuse yourself from other people's narratives and embolden yourself with this calligraphy style to write your own.

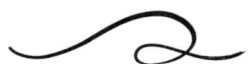

Calligrapher's Desk

STYLE: Engraver's Old English

FEELS LIKE: *reputation*

STATEMENT: Be bold and be heard

PEN: Calligrapher's pen with a 3–4mm chisel nib

BLACKLETTER varies in complexity, but Engraver's Old English is focused on impact. Hold your pen at a 45-degree angle so that if you just pressed the tip to the paper, it would make a forward slash: /. In other words, hold the pen so that the pointed edge of the tip is positioned at the 9 o'clock mark. Rather than a breezy, flowing script that flows across the page, this calligraphy style is straightforward but requires scrutiny, just like a headline. Hold your pen firmly, with a steady grip, and make your letters with careful, methodical strokes.

ABCDEFGHI
JKLMNOPQR
STUVWXYZ
abcdefghij
klmnopqrst
uvwxyz

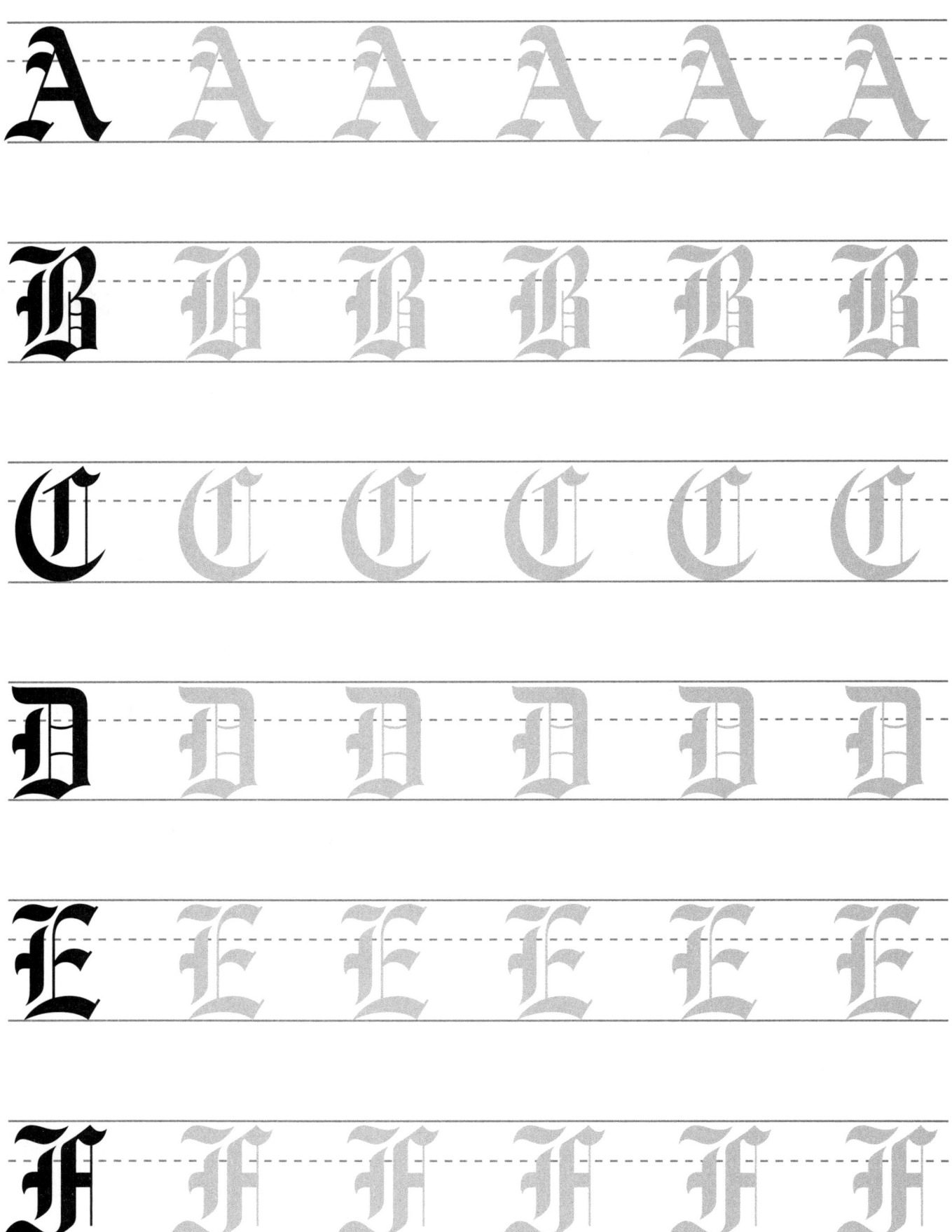

G G G G G G

H H H H H H

J J J J J J

J J J J J J

K K K K K K

L L L L L L

M M M M M M M

N N N N N N N

O O O O O O O

P P P P P P P

Q Q Q Q Q Q Q

R R R R R R

S S S S S S

T T T T T T

U U U U U U

V V V V V V

W W W W W W

X X X X X X

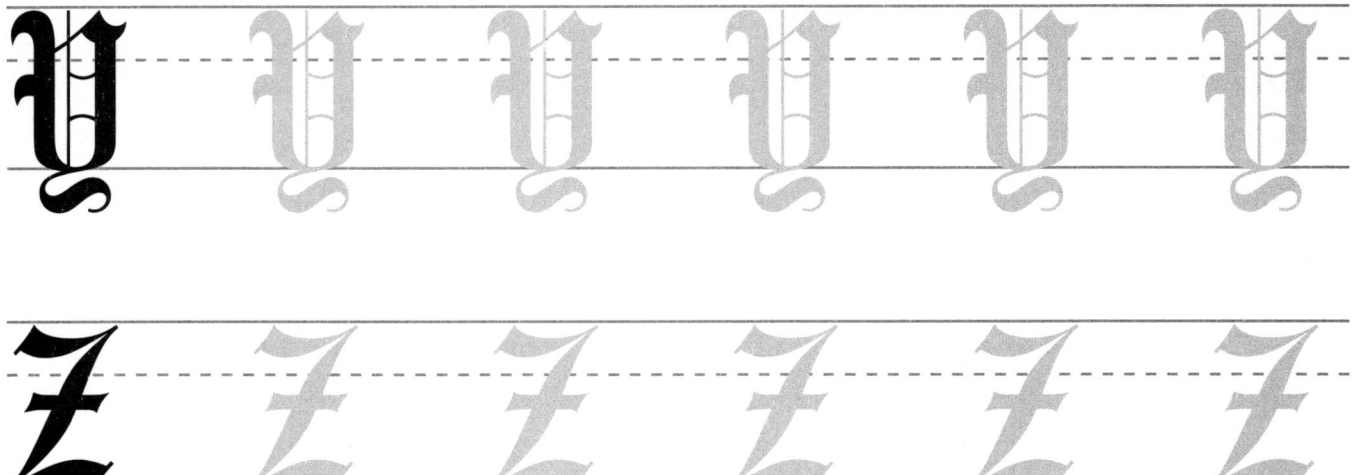

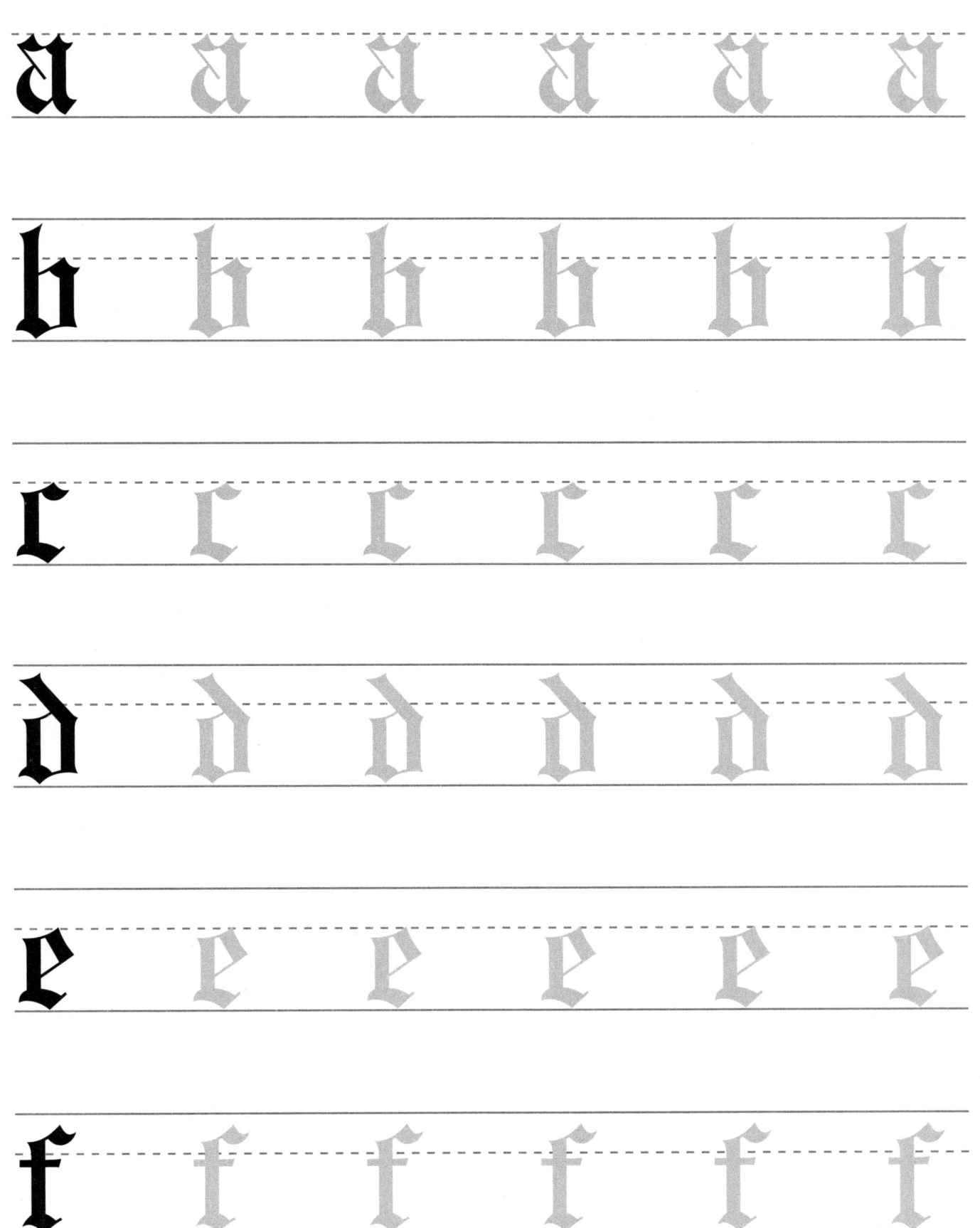

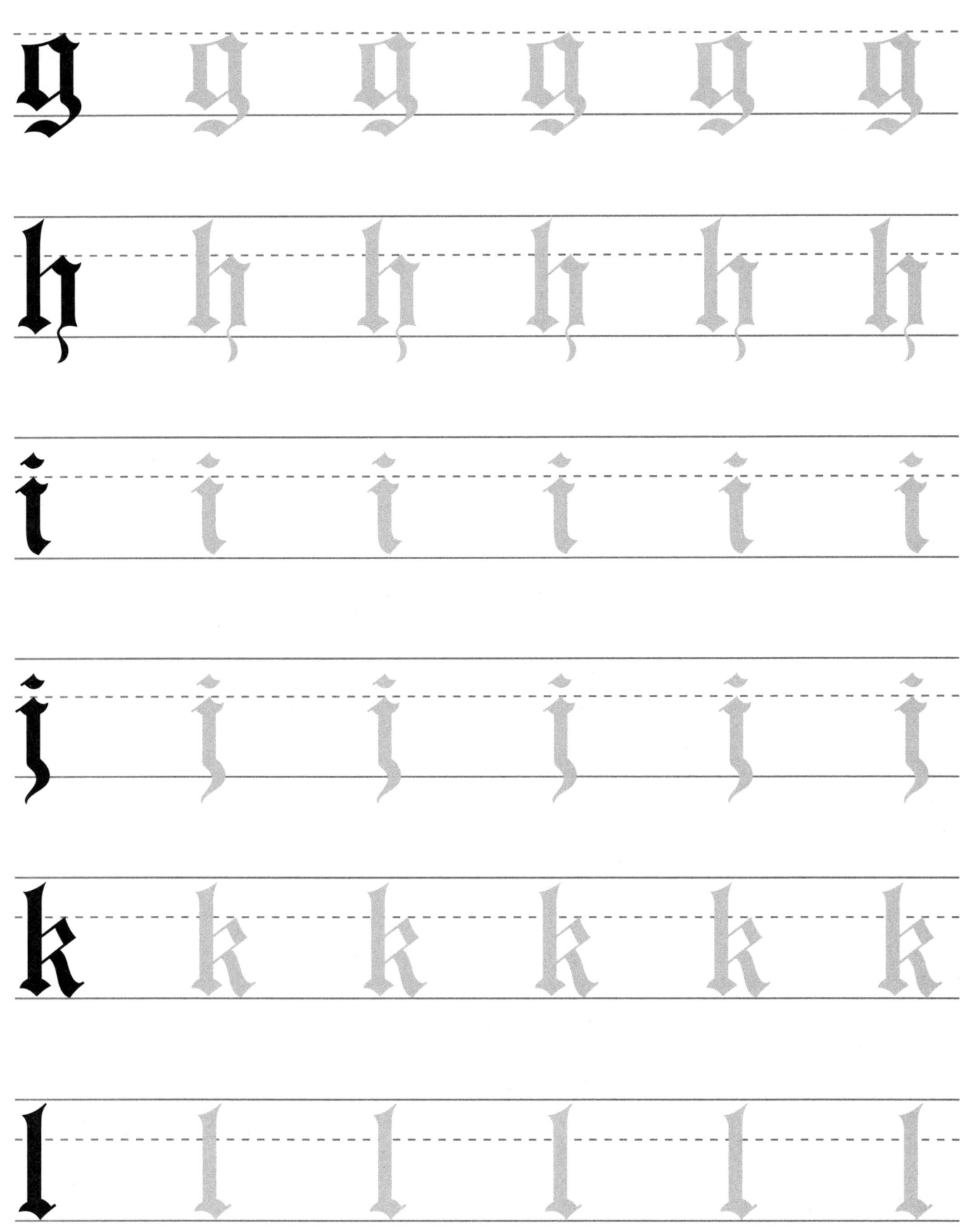

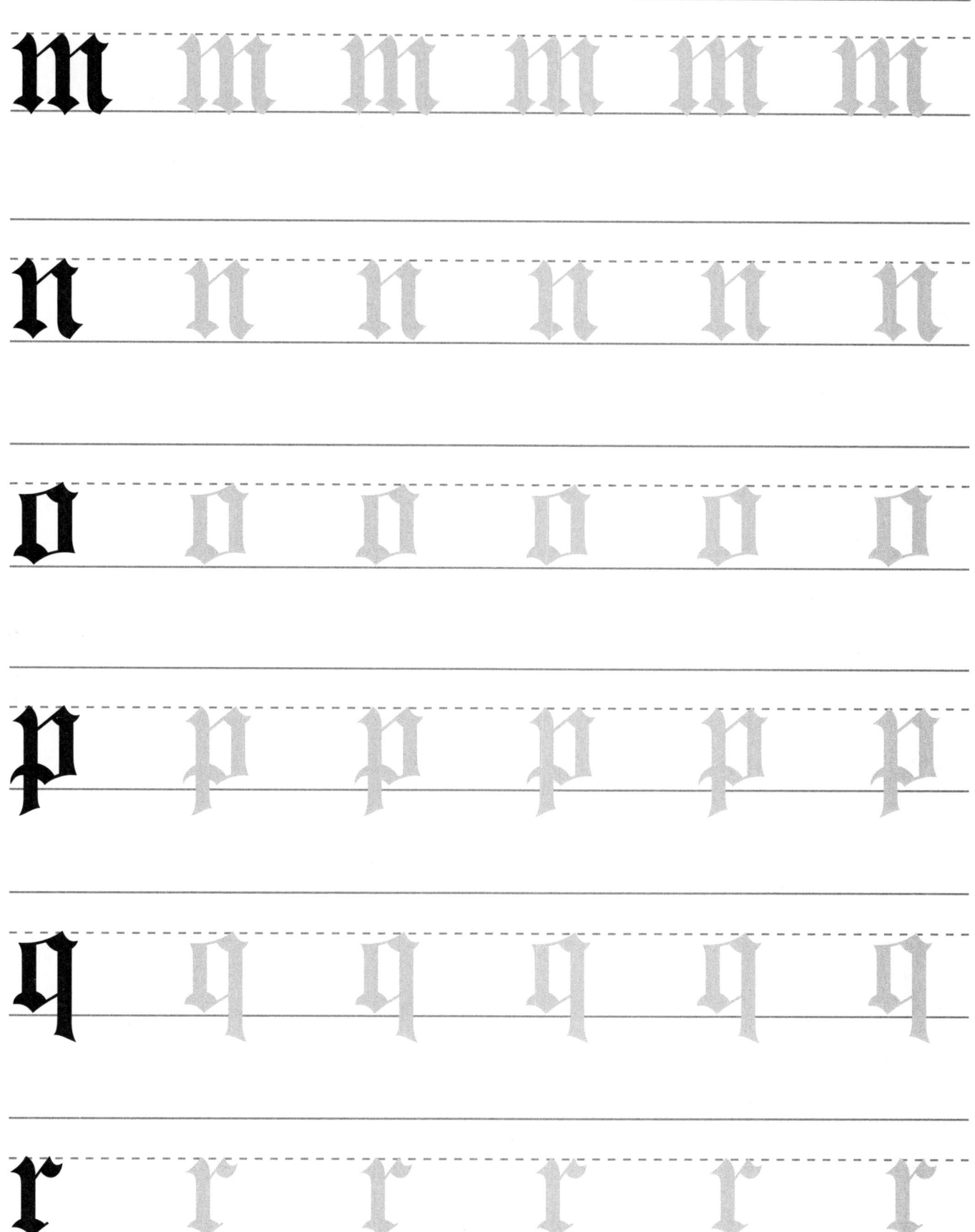

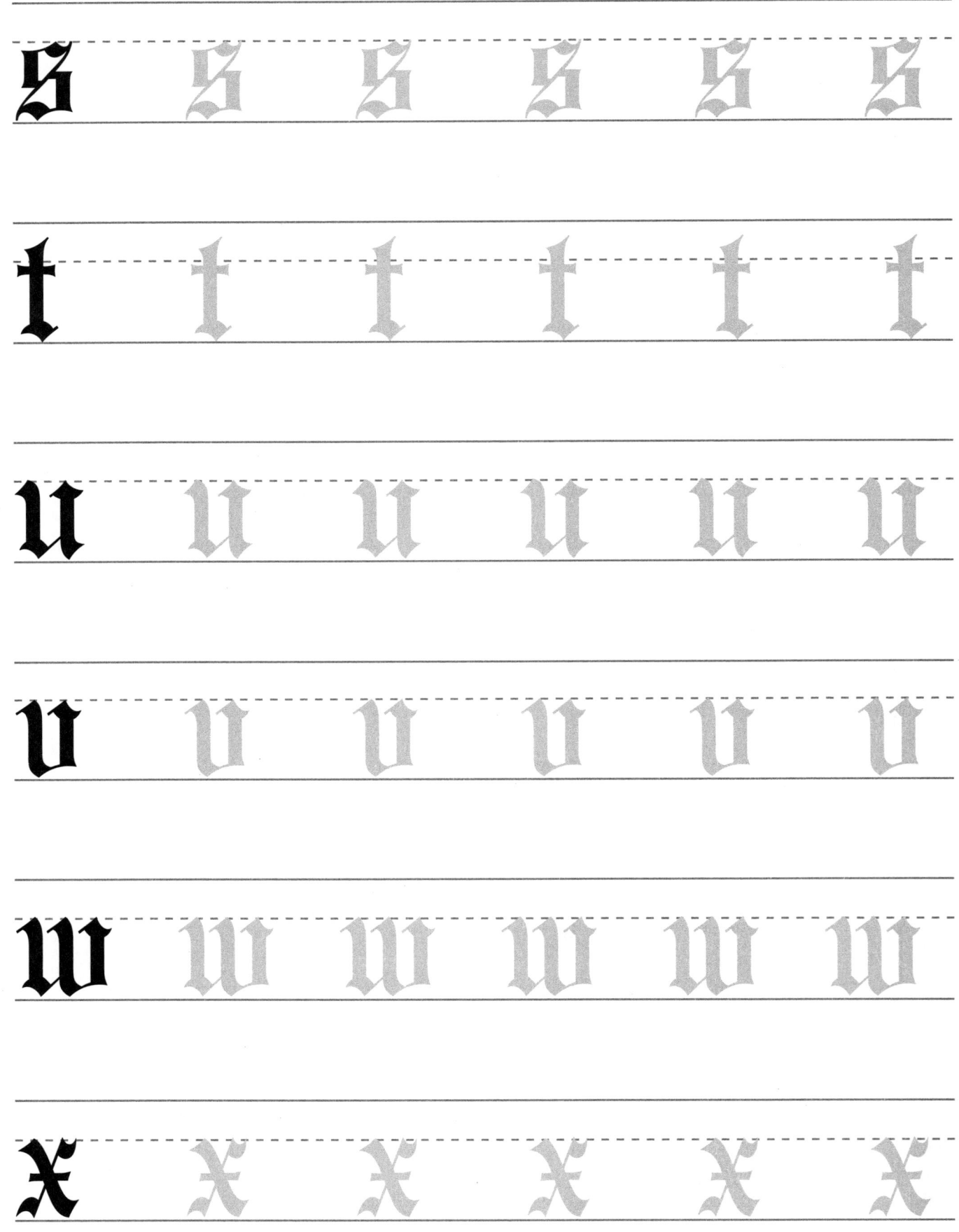

y y y y y y y

z z z z z z

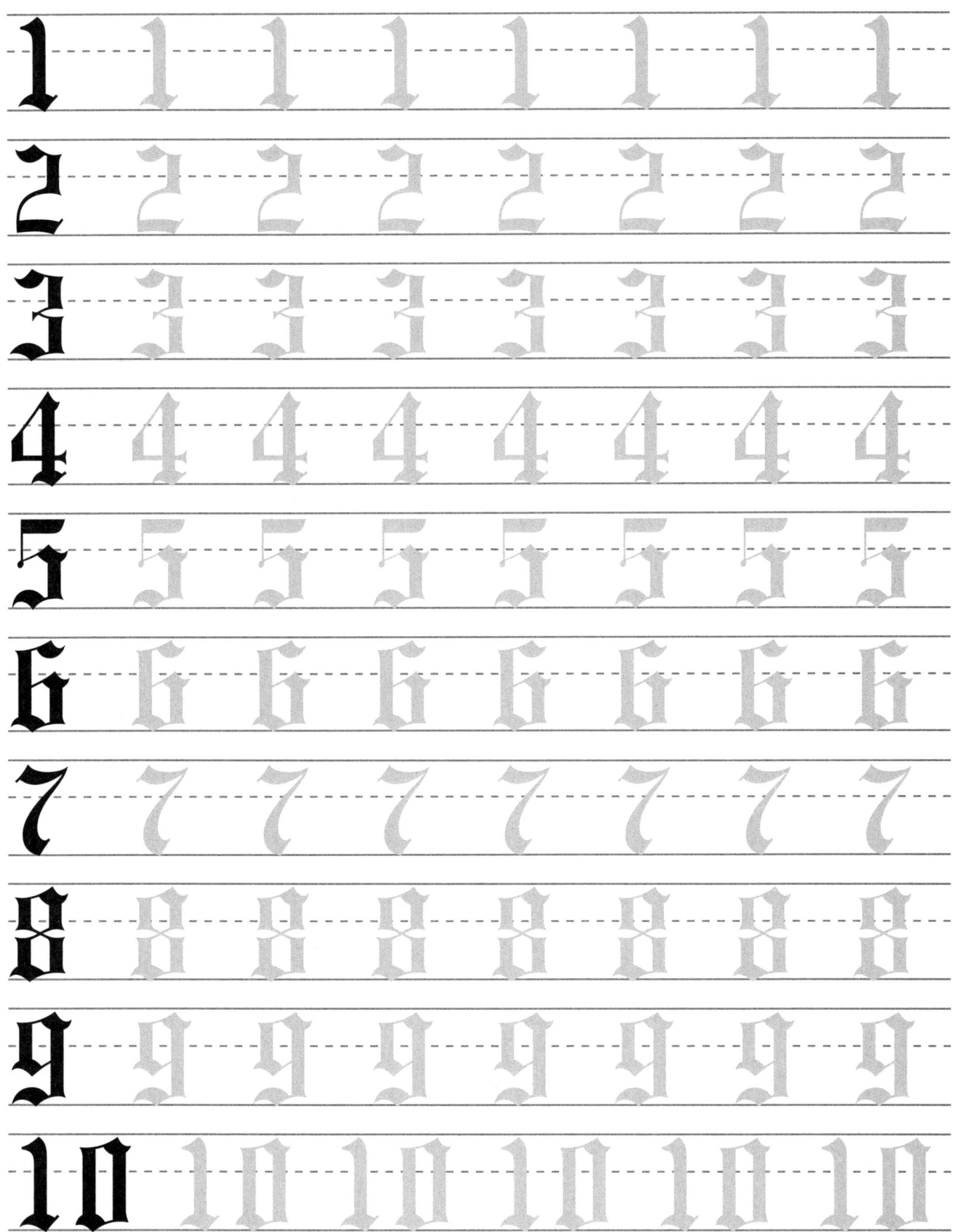

big reputation

big reputation

big reputation

big reputation

big reputation

big reputation

. . . READY

FOR IT?

. . . READY

FOR IT?

. . . READY

FOR IT?

already in my

getaway car

already in my

getaway car

already in my

getaway car

SNAKESKIN

& DIAMONDS

SNAKESKIN

& DIAMONDS

SNAKESKIN

& DIAMONDS

I did
something bad

I did

something bad

I did

something bad

Delicate &

Gorgeous

Delicate &

Gorgeous

Delicate &

Gorgeous

Don't Blame Me

Don't Blame Me

Don't Blame Me

Don't Blame Me

Don't Blame Me

Don't Blame Me

no explanation,
just reputation

no explanation,

just reputation

no explanation,

just reputation

This Is Why We Can't
Have Nice Things

This Is Why We Can't

Have Nice Things

This Is Why We Can't

Have Nice Things

This Is Why We Can't

Have Nice Things

King of My Heart

King of

My Heart

King of

My Heart

Lover Script

Promise you'll never find a script like me!

LOVER CAPTURES A KALEIDOSCOPE OF PASTEL DAYDREAMS, where Taylor's snakes transform into butterflies and her reputation can rest easy while she basks in the "afterglow." This album is Taylor at her most romantic and playful, and the Love Pro script is a perfect match. Its flowing lines and breezy attitude are charming enough for grand gestures, like love letters or hitting the road on some London Boy's scooter.

Working with Love Pro is all about going with the flow. There's no need for perfection—just let the brush glide smoothly across the page as easily as if you were drawing hearts and initials on a notebook. Perfect for casual projects, glittery journal entries, or heartfelt messages, this script transforms every word into a sparkling expression. Whether you're feeling Miss Americana's bright confidence or finding out that "it's nice to have a friend" and want to show it, Love Pro is by your side.

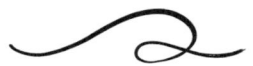

Calligrapher's Desk

STYLE: Love Pro

FEELS LIKE: *Lover*

STATEMENT: Light pink sky, no curfew

PEN: Medium-tip brush pen

LOVE PRO'S style is light and casual, and writing it requires a relaxed yet steady approach. Keep your pen at a slight angle—somewhere between 30 and 45 degrees—so that your strokes have a natural, gentle curve. Unlike rigid calligraphy scripts, Love Pro's letters flow smoothly with a light touch, like Taylor's butterflies springing from their cocoons. Let your hand move easily, maintaining even pressure and a loose wrist, so that your lines stay playful and consistent throughout the script.

A B C D E F G

H I J K L M N

O P Q R S T U V

W X Y Z

a b c d e f g h i j

k l m n o p q r s t

u v w x y z

A A A A A A A

B B B B B B B

C C C C C C

D D D D D D

E E E E E E E

F F F F F F

G G G G G G G

H H H H H H H

I I I I I I I

J J J J J J J

K K K K K K K

L L L L L L L

M M M M M M M M M

N N N N N N N N

O O O O O O O

P P P P P P P

Q Q Q Q Q Q Q

R R R R R R R

S S S S S S

T T T T T T

U U U U U U

V V V V V V

W W W W W W

X X X X X X

Y Y Y Y Y Y Y Y

Z Z Z Z Z Z Z

a   *a*   *a*   *a*   *a*   *a*

b   *b*   *b*   *b*   *b*   *b*

c   *c*   *c*   *c*   *c*   *c*

d   *d*   *d*   *d*   *d*   *d*

e   *e*   *e*   *e*   *e*   *e*

f   *f*   *f*   *f*   *f*   *f*

g   g   g   g   g   g

h   h   h   h   h   h

i   i   i   i   i   i

j   j   j   j   j   j

k   k   k   k   k   k

l   l   l   l   l   l

m   m   m   m   m   m

n   n   n   n   n   n

o   o   o   o   o   o

p   p   p   p   p   p

q   q   q   q   q   q

r   r   r   r   r   r

s   s   s   s   s   s

t   t   t   t   t   t

u   u   u   u   u   u

r   r   r   r   r   r

w   w   w   w   w   w

x   x   x   x   x   x

y y y y y y y

z z z z z z z

1   1   1   1   1   1   1   1

2   2   2   2   2   2   2   2

3   3   3   3   3   3   3   3

4   4   4   4   4   4   4   4

5   5   5   5   5   5   5   5

6   6   6   6   6   6   6   6

7   7   7   7   7   7   7   7

8   8   8   8   8   8   8   8

9   9   9   9   9   9   9   9

10   10   10   10   10   10

Cruel Summer,

Fever Dream

Cruel Summer,

Fever Dream

Cruel Summer,

Fever Dream

I'm the Man

I'm the Man

I'm the Man

I'm the Man

I'm the Man

I'm the Man

Miss Americana &

The Heartbreak Prince

Miss Americana &

The Heartbreak Prince

Miss Americana &

The Heartbreak Prince

Death By a
Thousand Cuts

Death By a

Thousand Cuts

Death By a

Thousand Cuts

You Need to
Calm Down

You Need to

Calm Down

You Need to

Calm Down

It's Nice to

Have a Friend

It's Nice to

Have a Friend

It's Nice to

Have a Friend

I Forgot That

You Existed

I Forgot That

You Existed

I Forgot That

You Existed

Soon You'll

Get Better

Soon You'll

Get Better

Soon You'll

Get Better

Daylight &

Afterglow

Daylight &

Afterglow

Daylight &

Afterglow

Pastels &

Paper Rings

Pastels &

Paper Rings

Pastels &

Paper Rings

folklore and *evermore script*

Write this down

THERE'S A QUIET MAGIC IN THE INTERTWINED WORLDS OF *FOLKLORE* AND *EVERMORE*—TWO ALBUMS WITH AN INVISIBLE STRING THAT CAPTURE THE AUTUMNS OF MEMORY AND HEARTACHE. Taylor's storytelling creeps into your senses like ivy, making IM Fell DW Pica Italic calligraphy script a perfect companion. With its graceful slant and classic serifs, this typeface captures the timeless, introspective feel of Taylor's twin albums, adding a literary elegance that elevates every word.

This script isn't hurried or loud. The magnetism of IM Fell DW Pica Italic lies in its simplicity, and its willowy presence asks you to slow down and let each stroke settle like falling leaves in the woods. Use it to keep your secrets, enrich your spaces, or adorn thank you notes. Let this font be "the 1" that acts as the backdrop to your stories.

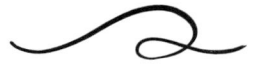

Calligrapher's Desk

STYLE: IM Fell DW Pica Italic

FEELS LIKE: *folklore* and *evermore*

STATEMENT: Long story short

PEN: Medium-tip brush pen

This **IMPACTFUL** calligraphy style gleams and glistens on the page. Hold your pen at a gentle angle, letting the fine strokes bring out epiphanies, hoaxes, and illicit affairs. The font's slight tilt and precise serifs invite a measured pace, turning every word into something worthy of being saved. Take up space and time with this gorgeous lettering style.

ABCDEFG
HIJJKLMN
OPQRSTU
VWXYZ

abcdefghij
klmnopqrst
uvwxyz

A A A A A A A A

B B B B B B B B

C C C C C C C C

D D D D D D D D

E E E E E E E E

F F F F F F F F

G G G G G G G

H H H H H H H

I I I I I I I

J J J J J J J

K K K K K K K

L L L L L L L

M M M M M M M M

N N N N N N N N

O O O O O O O

P P P P P P P

Q Q Q Q Q Q

R R R R R R R

S S S S S S

T T T T T T T

U U U U U U U

V V V V V V V

W W W W W W W

X X X X X X

r r r r r r

z z z z z z

a   *a*   *a*   *a*   *a*   *a*

b   *b*   *b*   *b*   *b*   *b*

c   *c*   *c*   *c*   *c*   *c*

d   *d*   *d*   *d*   *d*   *d*

e   *e*   *e*   *e*   *e*   *e*

f   *f*   *f*   *f*   *f*   *f*

g   g   g   g   g   g

b   b   b   b   b   b

i   i   i   i   i   i

j   j   j   j   j   j

k   k   k   k   k   k

l   l   l   l   l   l

m m m m m m m

n n n n n n n

o o o o o o o

p p p p p p p

q q q q q q q

r r r r r r r

S   S   S   S   S   S

t   t   t   t   t   t

u   u   u   u   u   u

v   v   v   v   v   v

w   w   w   w   w   w

x   x   x   x   x   x

y y y y y y y

z z z z z z z

1   1   1   1   1   1   1   1

2   2   2   2   2   2   2   2

3   3   3   3   3   3   3   3

4   4   4   4   4   4   4   4

5   5   5   5   5   5   5   5

6   6   6   6   6   6   6   6

7   7   7   7   7   7   7   7

8   8   8   8   8   8   8   8

9   9   9   9   9   9   9   9

10   10   10   10   10   10

Invisible String

Invisible String

Invisible String

Invisible String

Invisible String

Invisible String

my tears ricochet

my tears ricochet

my tears ricochet

my tears ricochet

my tears ricochet

my tears ricochet

Mad Woman

Mad Woman

Mad Woman

Mad Woman

Mad Woman

Mad Woman

Champagne

Problems

Champagne

Problems

Champagne

Problems

tolerate it

tolerate it

tolerate it

tolerate it

tolerate it

tolerate it

'tis the damn season

'tis the damn season

'tis the damn season

'tis the damn season

'tis the damn season

'tis the damn season

No body, no crime

No body, no crime

No body, no crime

No body, no crime

No body, no crime

No body, no crime

Right where you

left me. . .

Right where you

left me. . .

Right where you

left me. . .

Looking for my

willow coven

Looking for my

willow coven

Looking for my

willow coven

Story's Over, You're Still Writing Pages

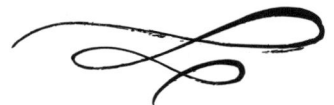

Practice your favorite styles here using

your favorite songs and eras!

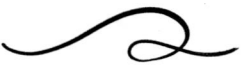

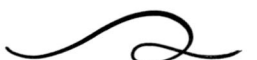